Joel Embiid

What YOU Can Learn from His AMAZING Life

By

Arthur Whitman

implied. Readers acknowledge that the author is not engaging in the rendering of legal, financial, medical or professional advice.

By reading this document, the reader agrees that under no circumstances are we responsible for any losses, direct or indirect, which are incurred as a result of the use of information contained within this document, including, but not limited to, —errors, omissions, or inaccuracies.

Other Books In This Series

Table Of Contents

Early Life

Joel Hans Embiid was born on March 16, 1994 in Yaoundé, Cameroon to Thomas and Christine Embiid. The family was comfortably upper middle class although Joel's father, who was a military officer, could be quite strict. For example, although the family had a maid, they would make Joel wash his own clothes as part of his chores. Another example is that before he could go outside and play sports Joel had to memorize that day's school lessons. Still, it was a loving home and Joel was happy.

Now, Cameroon is an African country filled with 23 million people. Their favorite sport, however, is not basketball, but soccer. In fact, when Joel was growing up, the entire country only had two indoor basketball courts! Cameroonians are absolutely obsessed with soccer. Everyone plays and a young Joel Embiid was no different. He was always cheerful in person but it hid an extremely competitive spirit. Joel, already taller than the other boys and extremely athletic, remembers how he would purposely turn his smile into a frown to help his team win.

SOCCER IS THE MOST POPULAR GAME IN CAMEROON, BY FAR.

"Let's say my team was down 2-0, I'd put my arms out and make this mean face and try to scare everybody. I kind of liked that they were afraid of me." – Joel Embiid on his soccer tactics.

With his height, Joel also played volleyball and was very good at it. In fact, his father had some hopes that Joel might be able to play volleyball professionally in Europe. Joel was fine with this, until everything changed for him. One day out of

7

the blue someone gave him a tape with some clips from the 2010 Celtics Lakers NBA finals featuring Kobe Bryant. For whatever reason, seeing this game stirred something deep within Joel. He wanted to play this game, but he didn't know how. Cameroon was all about soccer, not basketball.

The first experience Joel Embiid had of playing any kind of basketball was by himself shooting volleyballs at a rim. He was too embarrassed to share his dream with anyone, especially his strict father. However, as the saying goes, when the student is ready, the teacher will appear. For Joel, that teacher went by the name of Guy Moudio. Guy was one of the very few basketball coaches in all of Cameroon. He would often spend his days trying to find potential basketball players by watching soccer games. When he saw Joel, who was already so tall and obviously athletically gifted, he knew he had a prime candidate. The tricky thing was going to be convincing Joel's father to let him try.

You have to understand that Cameroon is not a very wealthy country and parents view sports in one of two ways. If a child shows some skill in soccer they will be encouraged to pursue the sport as there is a real possibility of being able to play in the various European professional leagues. Many Cameroonians, such as Semeul Eto'o and Alex Song, have already done this. If a child has a chance at turning professional he may not even have to go to school in order to practice and potentially follow in their footsteps. However, all other sports such as running track, handball and basketball are considered hobbies at best and a waste of time at worst. Whoever heard of someone making a living playing handball and just what is basketball anyway?

"Parents see Semeul Eto'o or Alex Song, and think, 'My son can do that.' With basketball, they don't see that. They might know (NBA player) Luc Mbah a Moute, but even he's not famous enough – some people don't know who he is." – Guy Moudio, Joel Embiid's first basketball coach.

As Joel suspected, his father was initially against the idea of him playing basketball. His father preferred the idea of Joel playing volleyball, as it was casual, low contact, and wouldn't interfere with his education. He wasn't convinced until Joe Touomou, who had played basketball at Georgetown and also saw the enormous potential that Joel possessed, told him, "*If you let him play basketball, he might not need to go to school. Someday, he might be able to buy his own school.*" Based on that, Joel's father let him play.

The first time Joel Embiid played an organized game of basketball he was, in the words of Guy Moudio, "terrible." At one point someone passed Joel the ball at mid-court and he just stood there. He literally didn't know what to do!
"What should I do, Coach?" asked Joel, as the other players swarmed around him.
"Pass the ball!" shouted Coach Moudio.
Joel passed the ball.

Although Joel was initially terrible, Coach Moudio had never had someone work as hard or improve as quickly as Embiid did. At one point someone gave Joel another tape that showed highlights of all of the great NBA centers from the 90's like David Robinson, Patrick Ewing and, most importantly, Hakeem Olajuwon. From that moment on Joel was hooked. He wanted to play basketball like those centers and Olajuwon was his idol.

Joel would practice the low post moves he had seen on that tape whenever he could and he was definitely getting better. However, he was still too embarrassed about his abilities to sign up for a local camp run by Cameroonian NBA player Luc Mbah a Moute. Guy Moudio registered him anyway, and Mbah a Moute couldn't believe the raw skill that young Joel Embiid displayed.

"The guard threw him a pass that was way ahead. Jo caught the ball, put it down, spun and finished on the other side of the rim in traffic. He'd been playing for six months. A normal person doesn't do that." – Luc Mbah a Moute.

At this point Joel's father still wanted him to play volleyball at the INSEP (National Institute of Sport and Physical Education) in France.

However, based on his performance and seemingly limitless potential, Joel had also been offered a chance to play basketball in the United States for the Montverde Academy. Montverde was Mbah a Moute's old school and offered Joel a full scholarship. Mbah a Moute explained to Joel's father that basketball was Joel's best option and, eventually, he agreed. Joel Embiid would continue his basketball education in the United States of America.

Although Joel was excited to be able to pursue his dream, it meant leaving his beloved family behind in Cameroon. At the airport there were tears all around as his parents, aunts and uncles, as well as two younger siblings, said good-bye. Joel's leaving wasn't easy on anybody.

"Just imagine walking away from your whole family like that. It's not easy." – Joel Embiid on leaving his family.

Despite the tears Joel didn't look back. He had a destiny to fulfill and that destiny was in America.

Learning Curve

When Joel Embiid arrived in America he was frankly nervous and afraid. Not only did he not speak English (he spoke French in Cameroon) but his entire family and all of the friends he knew were now on the opposite side of the planet. What's more, he was attending the Montverde Academy where he would be competing against players who had been playing basketball their whole lives. Joel had not even been playing basketball for a year at that point.

The first few practices were especially hard for Joel. The play was so fast compared to what he was used to that he could barely catch the ball. He would often trip over his own feet coming off of screens and bounce the ball off his foot when he tried to dribble. It wasn't easy, to say the least.

"I couldn't catch the ball. I got pushed around by everybody. I got my ass kicked every day." – Joel

Embiid on what the practices were like for him at Montverde Academy.

JOEL MODELS HIS GAME ON THAT OF NBA LEGEND HAKEEM OLAJUWON.

Not being able to speak English made it even harder for him. The first English phrase he learned was "Good morning." However, when he tried to use it the first time with his new teammates they all laughed at him. What was he going to do? The thought of giving up never entered his mind. Instead, Joel thought back to those times playing soccer in Cameroon when he would get in the opposing team's heads by acting fierce. Why couldn't he do that here? Instead of being intimidated, he was going to become intimidating.

"I was a little soft, but the Americans had no idea about any of that. They just knew I was from Africa. They thought I grew up poor, in the jungle, killing lions. I was like, 'If that's how they think of me, I'm going to use it'." – Joel Embiid.

Joel got to work. He continued to study the low post moves of his idol, Hakeem Olajuwon, six days a week and would practice them on his own whenever he could. Joel improved, and his battles with Montverde's other top center (and future NBA player for the Thunder) Dakari Johnson become legendary.

"Every day we fought. I had to make sure they stopped making fun of me. I had to let them know I came here for a reason." – Joel Embiid

Through hard work and dedication Joel learned English and his skill as a basketball player continued to grow by leaps and bounds. Joel was getting better and better and yet he had barely begun to scratch the surface of his potential. This was obvious to no one more than his coach at Montverde, Kevin Boyle. One time, when he had to eject Joel from practice for fighting with Dakari, he turned to the rest of the team and said, "Someday, you're going to be asking that guy for a loan."

By the end of his first year at Montverde Academy Joel had learned English and was making huge strides on the court. However, he still wasn't getting the playing time he craved so he transferred to The Rock School in Gainesville, Florida. It was there that he caught the eye of Norm Roberts, who was an assistant on the staff of Kansas Jayhawks head coach Bill Self. On Norm's recommendation Bill made the journey to Gainesville to see Embiid play. As they watched the game Norm tried to sell his coach on the idea of recruiting Embiid.

"I mean, I know he's raw. I know he's a project and all, but ..."

Bill Self immediately interrupted his assistant coach.

"Are you frickin' kidding me? This dude could be the No. 1 pick in the (NBA) draft. He can run. He's got good feet. He's got touch. He's unbelievable. He'll be the best big man we've ever coached if we can get him."

Bill Self was sold. He was willing to move Heaven and Earth for the chance to coach Joel Embiid.

The Jayhawks

Although many universities wanted to recruit
Joel, Bill Self and his Kansas Jayhawks were
ultimately successful. When Joel got there,
however, a familiar pattern emerged. Once again,
all of his teammates seemed to be so much more
advanced skill-wise than he was. He was getting
dunked on so often in practice that he asked to
be redshirted (this means he would practice
with the team but wouldn't play in games).
Coach Self convinced his prized freshman that
this wasn't necessary and things would be fine.
Just keep practicing.

As before, this is exactly what Joel Embiid did.
Bill Self gave him a tape of former Kansas
standout Jeff Whitney who was really good at
shot blocking. The next game Joel played in, he
blocked seven shots. He continued to study the
post moves of Hakeem Olajuwon and even
performed his famous "Dream Shake" against
New Mexico Lobos center Alex Kirk.

FOR A SINGLE SEASON, JOEL PLAYED FOR THE KANSAS JAYHAWKS.

"It comes easy to him. He moves like a 6-footer with his feet. He can move in a way that very few guys in the past have been able to move. There's a natural skill set there that very few 7-footers have." – Bill Self on Joel Embiid

Although Joel began the season on the bench, he soon cracked the starting lineup and began averaging 9.8 points, 6.5 rebounds, and 2.4 blocks in just twenty minutes of action.

What was a different for Joel at Kansas, as opposed to Montverde Academy, was that he could now speak English. What's more, the

Kansas fans loved him from the start and Joel loved them right back. Strangers would approach him and Joel would happily take pictures with them. He was always good for a quote so the local media loved him as well. This is when Joel's fun-loving personality really began to reveal itself to the wider world. At one point the media asked him if it was true that he had killed a lion with his bare hands. Joel wouldn't deny it and wore a mischievous smile while doing so. The media ate it up and his teammates loved it.

It looked like things were going really well for Joel. In fact, he was playing so well that Kansas was considered a favorite to win the NCAA championship and there was talk that Joel himself might go very high in the NBA draft, maybe even to number one. However, he endured a stress fracture in his back in March 2014, which prevented him from playing in the NCAA Tournament. Later, at an NBA pre-draft workout in Cleveland, Joel heard an audible crack in his foot. It was later learned that he had broken the navicular bone in his right foot. Instead of talking about Joel's seemingly unlimited potential, the talk was now of his durability and whether he would ever play in the NBA.

Delayed Potential

Before his injuries the emerging consensus was that Joel had superstar potential and would likely be the #1 pick in the draft. After suffering two consecutive injuries, however, teams began to get nervous. Basketball insiders began to wonder if he was another Greg Oden, another talented center who had been selected #1 overall but had never been able to live up to his potential due to injuries. Everyone agreed that Joel had amazing potential, but he also came with what was seen as enormous risk. Which team would be willing to take that risk?

On the day of the draft the Minnesota Timberwolves had the first pick and decided the risk wasn't worth it. They selected Joel's teammate Andrew Wiggins with the first pick overall. Next was the Milwaukee Bucks. They also passed on Joel's potential and went with Duke forward Jabari Parker. Next in line was the Philadelphia 76ers with the third pick overall. What would Philadelphia do?

FORMER 76ERS GM SAM
HINKIE, ARCHITECT OF "THE
PROCESS"

At this time Philadelphia had a general manager
by the name of Sam Hinkie. The year before, Sam
had begun a complete rebuild of the 76ers by
trading every player he could for draft picks. The
plan was to build through the draft in order to
find those special players, players like Michael
Jordon or Lebron James, who can make a team

special. In the meantime, he would field a team made up of "diamonds in the rough." Prospects who might able to play in the NBA, but needed valuable NBA playing time in order to develop their skills. This strategy, which came to be dubbed "The Process," would mean that wins in Philadelphia would be few and far between for a few years. In Sam's view, however, this process was necessary in order to build a solid foundation for the future. The question was though, would Sam select Joel as part of the process?

To Hinkie, this question was a no-brainer. Before he had entered the sports world, Sam had been involved in finance. In that business the goal is to buy low and sell high. To Sam Hinkie's way of thinking, Joel was an undervalued asset with huge future potential. He made the call to draft Joel Embiid with the third overall pick in the draft.

Now that Joel was a 76er, the next step was to set up a plan to heal his body so he could play again. It was decided that Joel would miss the entire 2014-15 season in order to focus on rehabilitating and strengthening his body. Management also wanted him around the team at all times, home and on the road, so that he would not feel isolated. They even acquired Luc Mbah a Moute to mentor Joel. It seemed like a good plan. However, the one person Sixer management didn't consult with was Joel himself.

The rehab work Joel did was extremely hard, and Joel quickly got tired of it. What was worse though was that they were forcing him to attend every Sixer game. He loved basketball and desperately wanted to play. However, he couldn't. Imagine there is something that you desperately want to do, that is so close that you could touch it, but you can't. These were the emotions that Joel was feeling and it was really hard on him.

"You're sitting there, we're losing, and you can't do anything. It was the worst." – Joel Embiid on being forced to watch games he couldn't play in.

Joel was able to watch the team play, but he couldn't participate, so he didn't really feel like he was part of the team. What's worse was that his rehabilitation prevented him from running and, as a result, his weight shot up. As a 20-year-old young man he didn't know how to drive and he really had nothing to do. Sometimes he would go for a walk and sneak into a nightclub where he would order his favorite drink, a Shirley Temple. However, when you're seven feet tall it's hard to remain inconspicuous and inevitably people would come up and ask him about his rehabilitation. Joel was frustrated about it and didn't really want to talk about it. He would usually just leave and return to his apartment on the fortieth floor, alone.

"He was locked up, he was all bottled up." – Brett Brown on what Joel Embiid was going through.

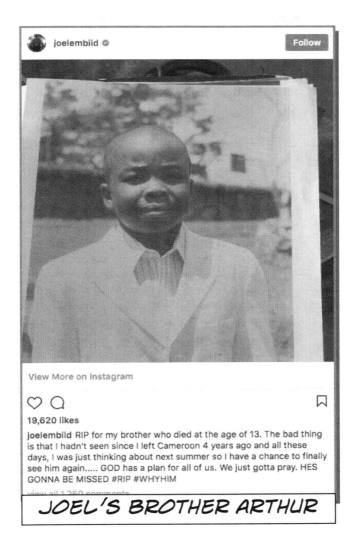

JOEL'S BROTHER ARTHUR

As frustrating as things were for Joel, things
were about to get worse. On October 16, 2014,
Joel's beloved younger brother Arthur was killed
in a freak car accident. A car lost control and ran
over Arthur in a schoolyard. The news hit Joel

27

like a ton of bricks. Arthur was a kind boy who would hand out crosses and donate his toys to the poor. How could something so horrible happen to a young boy like that? What was worse was that Joel felt guilty as he hadn't seen his brother for over four years as he pursued his basketball dream. After the accident, he would often find himself crying and praying by his bed at night. He would pray that his injured foot would heal and for his dearly departed brother. He couldn't help but ask himself, "Why me?"

With the help of his teammates, family and friends, Joel was able to get over the passing of his brother. He would never forget Arthur, but for the living, time marches on. And with the march of time Joel was starting to get some good news. His foot appeared to be healing. This became apparent when in May of 2015 he was allowed to step on the court and play some games 3 on 3. Joel took on all comers and basically destroyed them, including Philadelphia's other highly touted center, Nerlens Noel.

"I played against him and actually, I killed it." –
Joel Embiid on playing against Nerlens Noel.

Word spread quickly how well Joel had played.
The news even reached General Manager Sam
Hinkie, who was scouting players in California at
the time. Hinkie was excited, but cautious. Could
the hype be true? He texted Sixer forward
Robert Covington to confirm that what he was
hearing was true. Robert confirmed that it was.
Joel was amazing.

"[Embiid] literally almost ran all of our bigs out of
the gym. It was the first time I'd seen him, and for
him to dominate like that, it was like, 'Well,
damn.'" – Robert Covington on seeing Joel play
basketball for the first time.

The good news and buzz continued to grow
when Joel travelled to California to play some
pick-up games in Los Angeles. NBA guard Jamal
Crawford couldn't believe how good Joel was,
especially after such a long layoff.

"It was a joke how good he was. I saw then that the league had nothing for him." – Jamal Crawford

Things appeared to finally be going Joel's way. However, those feelings were short-lived when he was given some devastating news. A routine MRI revealed that his foot had stopped healing as expected. He was going to have to undergo a second foot surgery.

When the news hit, Joel became the focus of some extremely critical media attention. Stories of how he had been eating poorly and not always following the rehabilitation protocols that had been set for him started to come out. Most damning, in some people's eyes, were stories of Joel not always wearing the special medical boot that was supposed to aid in the healing process. It got to be so bad that Joel even considered quitting the NBA and returning to volleyball. "I wanted to get away from all of this drama and stay away," remembers Embiid.

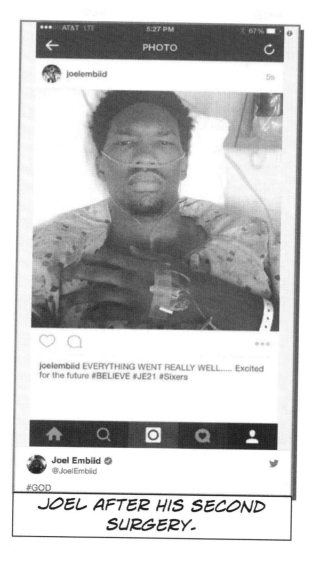

JOEL AFTER HIS SECOND
SURGERY.

To his coach, however, Joel's actions and what he was going through were not entirely a surprise. Although NBA players look larger than life, they are still young men filled with the frustrations and passions that all young adults share. Joel had been through a lot, from not being able to play the game he loved to losing his little brother to constantly being in the media spotlight. He hadn't been perfect, but who among us can claim to be perfect, particularly when we're twenty-one?

"Joel is a maverick. He's curious. He's competitive. Those qualities are going to allow him to maximize his very evident gifts. But when he was out, those qualities sometimes made it a challenge to always walk that Boy Scout's line." – Sixer's head coach Brett Brown

What Brett Brown realized was that this setback was likely to scare Joel a little bit. One of the illusions of youth is that you are invincible and that things will always turn out well. The MRI was the first time that Joel had to face the reality that in life this isn't always true.

"Appropriate fear had to creep in. 'Maybe I'm going to struggle to play basketball. Maybe there isn't a light at the end of the tunnel.'" – Brett Brown

Brett Brown was right. The second surgery did scare Joel, but Sixer management also realized they weren't blameless either. For Joel's second surgery Sam Hinkie brought in renowned sports scientist David Martin and together they developed a new plan. First of all, they asked for Joel's input and he made it clear that constantly having to watch the games when he couldn't play made him very unhappy. From then on Joel would be allowed to watch the games from Hinkie's personal suite whenever he wanted. Next, they got him a mentor in former NBA center Zydrunas Ilgauskas who had successfully rehabilitated the exact same kind of injury. Finally, they sent him to a world-renowned training facility in Aspetar, Qatar. There, in the sanctuary of this city on the other side of the world, Joel could focus on training, on his diet, and on getting a regular sleep schedule. Even better, he could do all of this free from the glare of the American sports media. The new plan was a success, and Joel Embiid was ready to make his long-delayed NBA debut for the 2016 – 2017 season.

The NBA

Joel Embiid made his long-awaited NBA debut against the Boston Celtics in a preseason game. For health reasons, the plan was to limit his playing time to twelve minutes. Embiid was nervous and excited at the same time, and he actually missed his first three shots. From there though he made his first shot and played well from then on. He finished the game with 6 points, 4 rebounds and 2 blocks.

"I thought he looked fine. He always wants to play more than the doctors tell him he can. I'm glad we played him like we played him. I thought that physically, he looked good." – Brett Brown on Joel's first NBA (preseason) game.

Joel made his regular season debut against Oklahoma City Thunder in Philadelphia. The crowd went crazy when Embiid was introduced and a group of fans held up a sign that said, "In Embiid We Trust." Although the Sixers lost the game due to a spectacular performance by

Oklahoma City guard Russell Westbrook (he scored 32 points and pulled down 12 rebounds), everyone was impressed with Joel. By the end of the game Joel had managed to score 20 points, grab 7 rebounds and had 2 blocks in only 25 minutes of action.

Joel continued to play well and there was talk that he might even make the All-Star team. However, this all came to an end when he suffered yet another injury, this time a meniscus tear in his left knee. Despite this he was named to the NBA all rookie first team.

Embiid began his second season in the NBA by signing a five-year, $148 million dollar extension. Despite his injury-plagued past, the Philadelphia 76ers believed in him and their faith was soon rewarded. In the 76ers season opener against the Washington Wizards Embiid had 18 points and 13 rebounds. Later, he scored a career high of 46 points and grabbed 15 rebounds in a victory over the Los Angeles Lakers. He also had seven assists and seven blocked shots, making him the first NBA player to post statistics like that since former Sixer legend Julius Erving had done it in 1982. Joel was also named as a starter in the NBA All-Star Game and was able to help the Sixers get into the NBA playoffs for the first time in six years. How far will the Sixers go? No one can know for sure, but the future does appear to be very bright for this young team with its young center, Joel Embiid.

Fire and Ice

Joel Embiid is not the only young superstar that the Philadelphia 76ers possess. The other is their 6-foot-10 point guard, Ben Simmons. If Embiid is the sun in the Sixers solar system, Embiid is the moon. Whatever success the Sixers have as a team in the future will be largely determined by how their two young stars mesh. Thankfully for Embiid and Simmons, that doesn't seem to be a problem.

JOEL EMBED AND BEN SIMMONS ARE
THE FUTURE IN PHILADELPHIA

In personality and background, Ben Simmons is almost the complete opposite of Joel Embiid. Whereas Joel is fun loving and expressive, Ben tends to keep to himself and has a natural quietness about him. "Night and day," said Sixer's swingman Justin Anderson when asked to compare the two, "Night and day."

Whereas Joel didn't discover basketball until he was fifteen, Ben was practically born with a basketball in his hand. The youngest of six children, Ben's older siblings would roll a basketball at him and have him roll it back when he was six months old. He started dribbling a basketball almost as soon as he was able to walk. His father, Dave, was a professional basketball player in Australia and would often take young Ben to practice when his wife had to work. Even when he was seven years old Ben wanted to practice with his dad and couldn't understand why he wasn't allowed to. In his mind, he was a basketball player just like everyone else. Why couldn't he play?

Like Joel, he left Australia to play basketball in America and attended Montverde Academy also. After a year at LSU he was ready for the NBA where he was picked first overall by Philadelphia. Just like Joel, however, he suffered a foot injury and had to miss his first season with the team before eventually taking the league by storm in his second.

In the past, other great NBA tandems, such as Shaquille O'Neal and Kobe Bryant, have broken up due to mutual jealousy and infighting. Both Ben and Joel are determined for this not to happen to them and, based on their personalities, they are likely correct. Ben doesn't crave the spotlight like Joel does and seems content to play the role of a deadly Robin to Embiid's Batman. If they are able to maintain this level of mutual respect they should be one of the NBA's most dangerous duos for years to come.

"They have a role to play in each other's success. What interests me more than going out to dinner or being together off the court all the time is respect on the court. And the respect is generated because you look at somebody and know they care, know they work, know the team is in their best interest." – Brett Brown on his two star players and their relationship.

Social Media Star

One of the aspects that has made Joel Embiid a star is that he has proven to be a master at social media, particularly Twitter and Instagram. It all started when he was injured and had nothing to do. Embiid's first agent, Arn Tellum, initially hired a social media coach for Joel. This coach advised Joel to play it safe and tweet non-controversial things. This didn't sit well with Joel who just wanted to have some fun. He fired the coach and made his social media accounts his own.

"But unfortunately, I got hurt and I didn't have anything to do. I found social media was a way for me to open up and show the world who I was and also keep my name out there." – Joel Embiid

Joel, true to his fun-loving nature, immediately started to have fun. He asked pop star Rihanna out on a date and even tried to recruit Lebron James by using Twitter. His true claim to fame on social media though is probably that of a playful troll. The art of trolling is based on saying something provocative in order to get a reaction, and Joel Embiid has proven himself to be a master.

"I don't go over the line, but I feel like I'm always right there. I'm not doing it to hurt anybody's feelings or create a situation. I just think it's funny." – Joel Embiid on the art of the troll.

One of his most famous trolls is when he posted a picture on Instagram of him scoring over Los Angeles Lakers' rookie Lonzo Ball. He dominated the Lakers in that game, but he made it clear that he wasn't trolling Lonzo. Instead, he was trolling his father (also a master of media) by tagging the location as "Lavar, Fars, Iran." Lavar Ball loved the troll.

Joel uses the troll to rile up opposing fan bases and teams. This, in turn, inspires him to bring his A game. In the Los Angeles game I just mentioned, Joel probably had his best game ever scoring 46 points to go along with 15 rebounds,

7 blocks and 7 assists. Trolling creates energy that Joel loves to feed on.

"I love that stuff. That gets me going. That makes me want to score and block a shot and dive on the floor. That makes me want to make a great play. I hate when we go on the road and other trams don't really have fans who cheer ... I feel it makes me sleepy." – Joel Embiid

Another famous Joel troll occurred when the Sixers blew a 24-point lead against the former champion Golden State Warriors. Joel posted an image of himself jawing with Warrior forward Draymond Green. The caption read, "Now we know what it feels like to blow a big lead ... Gotta stay focused to get the job done. Great learning lesson and I also love playing against Draymond #TheProcess." That troll referred to how the Warriors had blown a 3 – 1 lead to the Cleveland Cavaliers in the previous NBA finals. Troll level ... 10. If you don't yet follow Joel on social media, you might want to start. He's hilarious.

**JOEL TROLLING GOLDEN
STATE'S DRAYMOND GREEN**

*"He loves to poke the bear - - he thrives on it. I've
never really seen anything like it. It's different, but
it works." – former Sixer guard Nick Stauskas.*

Random Stuff

He is very smart.

As a professional basketball player, Joel uses his mind to get better. If he sees a move he likes, he will watch it fifty times until he has it committed to memory. Then, he will practice it until the move is his own. One time he bumped into former Sixer General Manager Tony DiLeo at an airport and Joel picked his brain about all of the basketball transactions he had done. DiLeo couldn't believe how well Joel understood the lottery, the salary cap, and the patience it takes to turn young players into stars. This is why Joel Embiid "trusts the process." He understands professional basketball from the point of view of the game and also as a business.

He understands how fickle fame can be.

Right now, Joel Embiid is seen as a rising star and is very popular. Joel is self-aware enough though to realize that those same fans can turn on you in an instant. That's the dark side of fame.

That a player as young as Joel Embiid already knows this shows, once again, how smart he is.

"People love you in the beginning, but at some point, they're gonna start hating you. LeBron. Russell Westbrook. All the superstars. Even Steph. He's so likeable. He does nothing wrong, but some people still hate him. It just comes with the nature of it. I've seen it. I feel like I'm about to go through it. I think it's coming. People always want something new." – Joel Embiid

He appreciates what former general manager Sam Hinkie did for him.

Sam Hinkie was the general manager who took a chance on Joel and oversaw his rehabilitation. He was also there for Joel (along with Brett Brown and Luc Mbah a Moute) when Arthur died. Sam was replaced by current general manager Bryan Colangelo in 2016 when the NBA decided it could no longer tolerate Philadelphia's losing ways. However, a large part of the reason that the Sixers were still losing is because Joel had been injured for so long. Joel feels partly responsible for Sam being fired and, as a result, often tips his hat to him social media wise now and again.

"I don't care. To me it was like, we've gone through so much, and I get that Sam Hinkie wasn't the most loved in Philly, but that was the guy who drafted me. I still like him. He did a lot for me." – Joel Embiid

He doesn't drink.

Joel doesn't drink alcohol at all. His preferred liquid refreshment is the Shirley Temple, a very sweet drink made from soda, cherry and grenadine.

WANT TO MAKE JOEL EMBIID HAPPY? THEN MAKE HIM HIS FAVOURITE DRINK, THE SHIRLEY TEMPLE.

He loves to play tennis.

If you go out late at night, you might catch Joel playing tennis on the public courts across from the Schuylkill River. He often plays with 76er's

49

development coach Chris Babcock. Chris reports that Joel doesn't play a power game as you might expect. Instead, he's a finesse player and a drop shot artist. He has also been known to take on random players on the public courts from time to time.

He loves to play in noisy arenas.

Whether they are cheering for him or against him, Joel wants the fans to be loud. If he feels the crowd is too quiet he will often do anything in his power to egg them on.

"It's like Happy Gilmore out there. Most people like the place to be quiet when they're shooting. Jo's like, 'Come on, man, make some noise!" – Nik Stauskas

"Oh, he eggs the crowd on. He loves it." – Robert Covington

He is a big video game fan and is ultra competitive.

Embiid owns a PlayStation 4 and is often known to play well into the night. He even takes the system on road trips.

"When I play, I rarely lose, so it makes me feel good about myself. And I keep winning, winning, winning." – Joel Embiid

"I played [PlayStation] with him once and said I'll never do it again … he talks the most crap ever. … I wanted to throw the controller out of his apartment building." – Sixer guard T.J. McConnell

He is a student of the game.

Embiid has reached out to former Laker star Kobe Bryant on several occasions for advice. What he wanted to learn was where Kobe was able to get the confidence to shoot the ball thirty-plus times in a single game. What he learned was that Kobe didn't take those shots because he had no conscience, he took them because he knew he could make them. When everyone else was partying, Kobe Bryant was practicing. This made a big impression on Joel and is a big part of the reason he doesn't drink or go to parties very often. He likes to practice and studies classic NBA games like they're textbooks. He also watches his contemporaries like Karl-Anthony Towns, Giannis Antetokounmpo, Kristaps Porzingas and Anthony Davis. He does this as he knows he will likely have to battle them one day in the playoffs and he wants to be ready.

He's not afraid to stand up for his teammates.
Just like Joel and Ben Simmons before him, their 2017 top pick, Markelle Fultz, has had a tough time with a mysterious shoulder ailment that restricted his playing time. When appropriate, Joel was quick to defend his teammate and criticized Sixer management on how they had handled the situation. When the team was attempting to trade Sixer center Jahlil Okafor, Joel criticized how that was handled as well. Sixer management may not have appreciated this, but his teammates did.

"Having your teammates' back - - that's what I feel being a leader is." – Joel Embiid

Finding Your Passion

One of the most important things in life can be finding your passion. Why do you get up in the morning? What do you live for? What are you passionate about? Joel Embiid found his passion when he saw clips of Kobe Bryant playing basketball for the first time. What might your passion be? It's a hard question to answer, and only you can answer it. However, here are some tips that might guide you along the way.

What activities do you do that, when you do them, you seem to lose all track of time?
When you are so focused on doing an activity that you literally lose track of time, you are likely to be very passionate about it. It engages your "flow", which means you are able to focus on it without regard to time. It can be anything from playing video games to sports to reading. For Joel, basketball engages his "flow". What activities engage yours?

What sort of things do you spend money on to participate in?

If you care enough to spend money on an activity, you are likely quite passionate about it. Although he didn't have to, Joel would have spent whatever money he had to play basketball. What activities would you spend money on if you had to?

What activities do you do that you fear judgment in?

This one is a little odd, so hear me out. If you fear being judged on something, the likely reason for this is because you care deeply about it. It is core to your being so the idea of being criticized for it can be painful. Joel initially didn't want to play in organized basketball games as he was afraid he wouldn't be good enough, and he desperately wanted to be good. It was important to him. When something is part of your core identity you are likely to work at it that much harder as it is important to you. Art, poems, writing, songs … what have you ever created that you were nervous to show someone? If you're afraid to show it to someone, you are likely passionate about it.

Have you ever done anything that even the thought of doing it makes your heart race?
If you care about something so much that your heart literally elevates, you are likely passionate about it. You know this is true as your body is literally physically responding to it. Always take notice of anything that causes your body to react in this way.

One of the ills of modern society is that so many people are more interested in fitting in than standing out. They are not being true to themselves and, as a result, they are not happy. Joel could have fitted in by staying in Cameroon and playing soccer but he loved basketball. He stuck with it and look where it led him! Take your time to discover and cultivate your passions. You won't regret it!

Developing Grit

One of the biggest factors in being successful is developing the passion and perseverance to achieve very long-term goals. This personality trait is sometimes known as "grit" and social scientists are finding that it is a key factor in whether a person succeeds or fails at a given task. "Your 'I can' is more important than your 'IQ'" is the way Robin Sharma put it. Joel obviously showed tremendous "grit" when he overcame all of his injuries to play in the NBA. Part of the reason he was able to do this was because he was passionate about basketball. Well, we've already talked about some ways to discover your passion in the previous chapter. But how about the second part? Is it possible to develop your perseverance?

You can, if you follow what is known as the "Hard Thing Rule." The "Hard Thing Rule" states that you should try to do one thing that is somewhat difficult for you or out of your comfort zone every day. For example, let's say you want to be writer. The "Hard Thing Rule" in this case would be to resolve to write a little bit every day, even for only fifteen minutes. Another example would be if you wanted to get in better shape so you resolved to exercise for a bit every day. It can really be anything so long as it is a little hard for you and worthwhile. Sticking to things, even on those days when you don't feel like doing it, develops character and grit, just like Joel Embiid has.

Quotes

Embiid

"If somebody teaches me the point guard position, I feel like I'd be able to [play it]." – Joel Embiid

"When I moved here, I was a kid who didn't like to talk very much. I was calm and quiet, like my dad." - Joel Embiid on what he was like when he first moved to the US.

"@KingJames hey bro hope you're having a good day ... Want to join us in philly?? Peace" – Joel Embiid attempting to recruit Lebron James on Twitter.

"I hope I'm not gonna get fined already with those LeBron's tweets. Is it legal to recruit over Twitter @NBA?" – Joel Embiid

"I'm trying to be president in 25 years after basketball good idea or nah? Cameroon of course, not USA." – Joel Embiid

"I hate seeing y'all bashing KD. At least he cares about winning more than anything and that deserves some respect." – Joel Embiid defending Kevin Durant after he signed with Golden State.

"Since I've been in the league, I feel like they can't play." – Joel Embiid on why he doesn't watch college basketball anymore.

"I tweeted at her, and then one or two of my friends texted me and a lot of people on Twitter were like, 'Oh, she's married to Kanye! I was like, Oops! I gotta make sure to tweet that I didn't know she was married.'" – Joel Embiid

"You know how I learned to shoot? I watched white people. Just regular white people. They really put their elbow in and finish up top. You can find videos of them online." – Joel Embiid

"I was a little soft, but the Americans had no idea about any of that. They just knew I was from Africa. They thought I grew up poor, in the jungle, killing lions. I was like, 'If that's how they think of me, I'm going to use it.'" – Joel Embiid

"I don't know why but my game has gotten so much better in the past 2 years. I'm not the same guy." – Joel Embiid

"I just love winning. When I play, I rarely lose, so it makes me feel good about myself. And I keep winning, winning, wining." – Joel Embiid on his love for PlayStation

"Having your teammates' backs - - that's what I feel being a leader is." – Joel Embiid

"I want to get into the fans. I want to hear their voices and hear people talking s--- and hear people get into the game crazy and chanting 'Ref sucks' or 'Trust the process' or 'Joel, you suck!'" – Joel Embiid

59

"I love the pressure." – Joel Embiid

"Trust the Process." – Joel Embiid

NBA Players on Embiid

"He's going to be really good. I mean, he's already good, but he's going to be really, really good. As the games go on, you get more and more games, you get more of a feel for the games. He'll be a really good player in the league" – LeBron James

"He skilled. He can shoot the ball, put the ball on the floor, he's got great footwork." – John Wall

"Offensively, he's just skilled, man. He's probably the most skilled big man we have in this league, man. Shooting the 3 at a high level, 7-2, finishing about the basket, making plays for his teammates. And then defensively, he blocked my shot. He's everywhere, man. He has a bright future and Philly has got something special here." – James Harden

"For me as a fan, it's good to see him back out there. We need young guys like that as a part of this league." – Carmelo Anthony

"I like that kid a lot. (You know that) I don't give a lot of people props, but I like that kid a lot. I think he's got a great chance of being the best big in this league ... after I retire." – DeMarcus Cousins

"I played [PlayStation] with him once and said I'll never do it again. He talks the most crap ever … I wanted to throw the controller out of his apartment building." – T.J. McConnell

"He loves to poke the bear - he thrives on it. I've never really seen anything like it. It's different, but it works." – Nick Stauskas

NBA Coaches on Embiid

"Obviously both of those guys are very talented. I don't know Mr. Embiid like I know Mr. Duncan, so I don't know what makes him tick or what he's made of or what his character is like. But if that character, that hunger, that work ethic and that maturity exists, he and Brett will be a great match." – Spurs coach Gregg Popovich

"He's different than anybody that's been in this league in a long, long time. He's a tremendous talent, he really is. I've never seen a guy that size, and with that kind of strength, that's got such a soft touch. He shoots the ball with the touch of like Steph Curry. It's so soft when it leaves his hand." – Pelicans coach Alvin Gentry

"Embiid's a big factor in there with his size, his abilities to clog the lane defensively, and then offensively to make you do things that you have to keep him out of the paint. He's long – he's going to finish in there." – Knicks coach Jeff Hornacek

"Embiid is a very special, talented player. If he was [still] playing, he probably would have run away with [rookie of the year] because he is a dominant player." – Bucks coach Jason Kidd

"I watched him when he was a 16-year-old, out of Gainesville growing up. The amount of strides he made in an 18-month stretch between that point and (when he attended) Kansas was incredible … He just has some gifts that other people don't have so he's got a real chance to be good, that's for sure." – Celtics coach Brad Stevens

"He was fantastic in those 31 games, head and shoulders above all the rest in those games." – Heat coach Erik Spoelstra

"He's hard to guard. He's herky-jerky. He's got a lot of Olajuwon in him." – Thunder coach Billy Donovan

"He's a 20-point a game guy who's only playing 25 minutes a game to get his 20 points. That's a high level of production in just over half the game. The guy's been tremendous. What can he not do?" – Pistons coach Steve Van Gundy

"We encourage him to explore and be a little unfiltered. That's how he lives. And that's how he plays." – Sixers coach Brett Brown

"He's one of these guys that, when you talk to him, he looks you in the eye and you wonder if he's really paying attention. But he really is. He's

listening to everything you say." – Kansas assistant Norm Roberts

Others

"Joel Embiid, he's great for the league. They [Embiid and Ben Simmons] gonna be monsters if they if they can stay healthy for the next 10 to 15 years." – Charles Barkley

"Really huge. He moves like Olajuwon. But he's huge. And he shoots 3's. We couldn't stop him. He almost won the game. He's huge. He's so huge. You gotta see him, he's huge. He's amazing. He's so huge." – Bill Simmons

"Embiid has the potential to be a star in the NBA." – Tim Legler

"He's been unbelievable as far as listening goes, we never have to tell him something twice." – Bill Self

Timeline

1994 – Joel Hans Embiid is born to Thomas and Christine Embiid on March 16, 1994, in Yaoundé, Cameroon.

2009 – Begins to play basketball at the age of fifteen. Is discovered by Luc Mbah a Moute at a basketball camp. Mbah a Moute immediately sees his potential and advises him to move the United States to become a professional basketball player.

2010 – Enrolls at Mbah a Moute's old school Montverde Academy in Florida.

2011 – Due to lack of playing time Embiid transfers to The Rock School, a Christian academy. He leads the school to a 33 – 4 record and the state championship.

2012 – Embiid is considered one of the top college recruits in the country and commits to playing for the Kansas Jayhawks.

2013 – Attends the University of Kansas for one year. Embiid suffers a stress fracture in his back, which prevents him from playing in the NCAA tournament.

2014 – On April 9, 2014, Embiid decides to forgo his final three years of college eligibility and declares for the NBA draft.

2014 – On April 15, Embiid is selected third overall by the Philadelphia 76ers.

2014 – August 26, Embiid signs his rookie contract. He is ruled unlikely to play at all in the 2014 – 15 season due to a broken navicular bone in his foot.

2014 – October 16, 2014 – Joel's younger brother, Arthur, dies in a car crash in Cameroon. He is thirteen years old.

2015 – June 13, it is announced that his foot has healed less well than expected. A second surgery is performed and Embiid misses the entire 2015 – 2016 NBA schedule as well.

2016 – On October 4, Embiid starts his first game as the center for the Philadelphia 76ers in the preseason.

2016 – On October 26, Embiid makes his debut as the starting center for Philadelphia in a regular season game. Playing under a minute's restriction he records 20 points, 7 rebounds and 2 blocks in 25 minutes of playing time.

2017 – On February 11, it is announced that Embiid will be out indefinitely with a torn meniscus in his knee.

2017 – On March 24, Embiid has minor arthroscopic surgery performed on his knee. Despite his limited playing time Joel is named to the NBA All-Rookie First Team.

2017 – On October 10, 2017, Embiid signs a five-year, $148 million dollar contract with the Philadelphia 76ers.

2018 – On January 18, Embiid is named a starter for the 2018 NBA All-Star Game.

Check Out These Great Books Too!

We're big fans of Funny Comics, who make both educational and entertaining stories for kids. Below are some samples of their work.

Viva La Revolution!

In this fully illustrated comic time travelling friends Big Buddy and Little Buddy help George Washington!

Tear Down This Wall!

In this fully illustrated short story time travelling friends Big Buddy and Little Buddy help Ronald Reagan tear down the Berlin Wall!

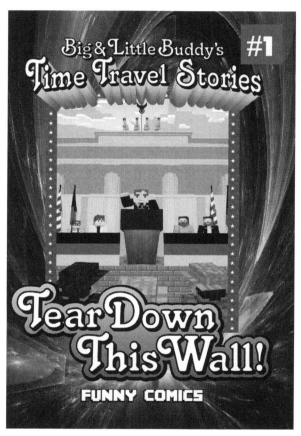

Apple Of My Eye

In this fully illustrated short story Big Buddy and Little Buddy help Steve Jobs launch the Apple II!

Jurassic Block

Funny Comics also has a series of parody comics based on famous movies like Jurassic Park, Star Wars and The Avengers

Diary Of A Friendly Creeper

In this series we follow the adventures of a creeper who doesn't want to explode, he just wants to be friends!

What Should Our Next Biography Be?

The biography you have just finished reading was on NBA star Joel Embiid. Who should we write about next? If you have any ideas, let us know! To do this, please consider leaving a review for THIS book on Amazon and let us know whom you would like to see be the focus of our next book. The review would really help us out and we really want to know who you are interested in reading about. So, let us know! Lily says thank-you in advance for helping us!

Made in the USA
Middletown, DE
25 January 2020